VISITING MY COMMUNITY

BANK

Piper Whelan

LIGHTBOX

Go to
www.openlightbox.com
and enter this book's
unique code.

ACCESS CODE

LBXV9353

Lightbox is an all-inclusive digital solution for the teaching and learning of curriculum topics in an original, groundbreaking way. Lightbox is based on National Curriculum Standards.

OPTIMIZED FOR

- ✓ TABLETS
- ✓ WHITEBOARDS
- ✓ COMPUTERS
- ✓ AND MUCH MORE!

STANDARD FEATURES OF LIGHTBOX

AUDIO High-quality narration using text-to-speech system

VIDEOS Embedded high-definition video clips

ACTIVITIES Printable PDFs that can be emailed and graded

WEBLINKS Curated links to external, child-safe resources

SLIDESHOWS Pictorial overviews of key concepts

INTERACTIVE MAPS Interactive maps and aerial satellite imagery

QUIZZES Ten multiple choice questions that are automatically graded and emailed for teacher assessment

KEY WORDS Matching key concepts to their definitions

VIDEOS

WEBLINKS

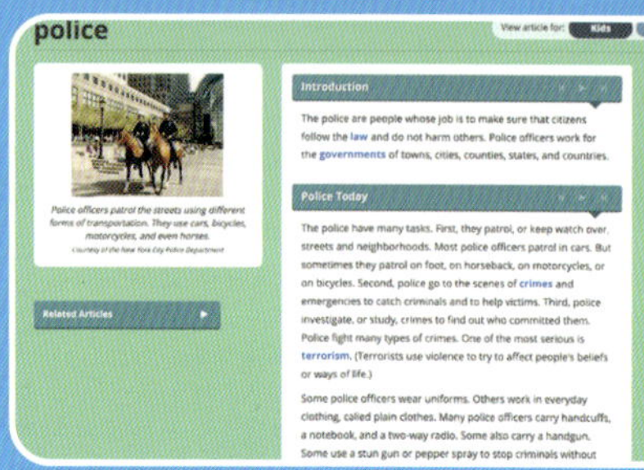

SLIDESHOWS

QUIZZES

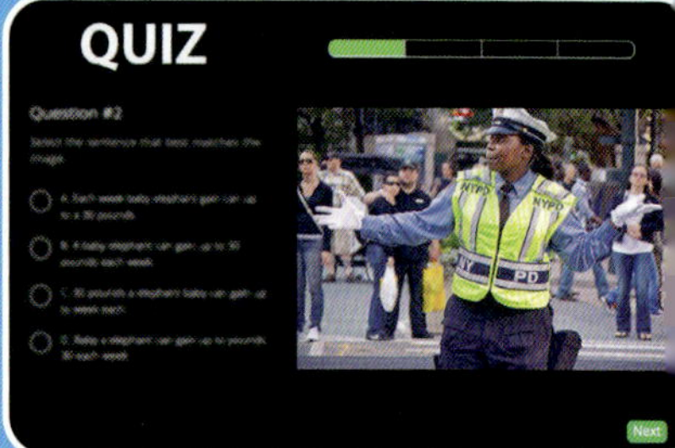

VISITING MY COMMUNITY

BANK

Contents

My community is where I live.

There is a bank in my community.

People put money in the bank. The bank keeps it safe.

The bank gives people an account to keep their money in.

Bank tellers work at the bank.

They help people take their money out.

Tellers count money to show it is the **right amount.**

The bank makes checks.

People use checks to give money to someone else.

Banks have machines. They are called ATMs.

People take money out of them.

People need **plastic cards** from their bank to use an ATM.

Banks help people go on trips.

The bank takes American dollars from people. It gives them money from other countries.

An American dollar bill only lasts **18 months** before wearing out.

100
Australia

Banks let people borrow money.

People can use this money to help buy a house.

Banks hold special events.

They raise money to help sick people.

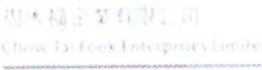

My class will visit the bank.

We will see how banks keep money safe.

What have you learned about the bank?

Which pictures show a bank?

KEY WORDS

Research has shown that as much as 65 percent of all written material published in English is made up of 300 words. These 300 words cannot be taught using pictures or learned by sounding them out. They must be recognized by sight. This book contains 51 common sight words to help young readers improve their reading fluency and comprehension. This book also teaches young readers several important content words, such as proper nouns. These words are paired with pictures to aid in learning and improve understanding.

Page	Sight Words First Appearance
4	I, is, live, my, where
5	a, in, there
6	it, keeps, people, put, the
7	an, gives, keep, their, to
8	at, help, out, right, show, take, they, work
10	makes
11	give, use
13	are, from, have, need, of, them
14	American, before, go, lasts, on, only, other, takes
16	let
17	can, house, this
20	will
21	how, see, we

Page	Content Words First Appearance
4	community
5	bank
6	money
7	account
8	tellers
10	checks
13	ATMs, cards, machines
14	bill, dollars, months, trips
18	events
20	class

Published by Smartbook Media Inc.
350 5th Avenue, 59th Floor, New York, NY 10118
Website: www.openlightbox.com

Library of Congress Control Number: 2020934514

ISBN 978-1-5105-5436-8 (hardcover)
ISBN 978-1-5105-5437-5 (multi-user eBook)

042020
110819
Printed in Guangzhou, China
1 2 3 4 5 6 7 8 9 0 24 23 22 21 20

Project Coordinator: John Willis
Designer: Ana María Vidal

The publisher acknowledges Alamy, Getty Images, and iStock as its primary image suppliers for this title.